The

BOLD
RETURN
of the
DUNCES

The

BOLD
RETURN
of the
DUNCES

WHEN PEOPLE ASK US "WHY ELLERSLIE?"
WE SAY "WHY DON'T YOU READ THIS!"

ERIC LUDY

Ellerslie PRESS
WINDSOR, COLORADO

Scripture taken from the King James Version®. Public Domain.

ISBN 9781943592074 (paperback)
ISBN 9781943592173 (ebook)

ELLERSLIE PRESS
655 Southwood Lane
Windsor, CO 80550
Ellerslie.com

Published in the United States of America.
First Edition, 2015
Second Edition, 2016

EricLudy.com

CONTENTS

THE AUDACIOUS MARCH DOWN BRICKBAT LANE

The "East End" of London in the mid-to-late 1800s was a place of darkness. Jack the Ripper roamed the streets of Whitechapel while poverty strode alongside him as if it were his lackey. Death, despair, drunkenness, and disease were more common than a cold, and it seemed hope was yesteryear's fancy. But, as is true in every season of darkness, God raises up a band of heavenly fools to shine the ancient Light of Truth. And so He did in East London. God commissioned the hallelujah-singing Salvation Army to start marching in the midst of this destitution.

This audacious band of soul-winners was not received with the august acclamation you would think that those despairing and in desperate need of hope would supply to their rescuers. Instead of acclaim, applause, and gratitude, they were met with grave hostility. Almost always a mob numbering in the thousands stood to block the way of the Salvation Army. And such was the case one day as the Army marched toward Sheffield, England. The shouts of "Kill 'em!" rang in the streets, a savage mob hooted, spat, screamed, cursed, hurled filth, refuse, and brickbats, and charged headlong at the humble band of Christian men and women with malevolent intent.

The motley band of marching saints was led by William Booth, who sat upon a carriage with an open top, fully exposed to the hurling debris. His wife, Catherine, was seated beside him. It wasn't the first time he had received this kind of reception. It wasn't the first time he had arrived at his destination bloodied and bruised. And it certainly would not be the last. Throughout history, "the bold return of the dunces" has never been received with applause or acceptance.

But amazingly, even amid the flying filth and the venomous insults, Booth and his followers seemed to have faces of angels. Looking closely, one might event detect the presence of genuine smiles playing on their lips.

Booth charged his followers onward, through the opposition. He commissioned them to not retaliate, but simply march on, beating their drums, playing their horns, and embracing the mockery. So they marched, singing at the top of their lungs, declaring to anyone who would listen that the Son of God had conquered sin and death on their behalf.

They finally arrived at their destination in the same way that all Christ's fools arrive — bruised, but blessed. Clothes torn, but hearts overflowing with love. Insulted, but shouting "Hallelujah!" Bloodied, but invigorated and ready to go right back out and do it all again.[1]

This scene clearly enunciates our vision for Ellerslie. We want to build up men and women ready to march down Brickbat Lane, straight through the venomous

---

1   Sallie Chesham, *Born to Battle: The Salvation Army in America*, p.21

mob, shouting "Hallelujah" at every malevolent attempt against their lives and dignity, unashamedly declaring the victory of Jesus Christ to all who will listen.

This is the Bold Return of the Dunces.

To be a fool is not something I would advise to anyone. But to become a "fool for Christ" is truly a noble pursuit. It is for this purpose that Ellerslie was founded. We are a school that exists to raise up fools for Christ.

For the Kingdom and the King's Glory,

Eric Ludy
Windsor, Colorado
May 2015

I.

FASHIONABLE IDIOCY

If I thought I could win one more soul to the Lord
by walking on my head and playing the tambourine
with my toes, I'd learn how!

William Booth

The tall pointy dunce cap has been a symbol of shame for centuries. To be the schoolboy stuck in the proverbial corner with the idiot's hat pressed down on his head is second in shame only to the idea of being paraded through the school hallways in one's underwear. As a result, the word *dunce* and the concept of "abject humiliation" have always been closely associated. And for those of us that are walking thesauruses, we are well aware that the word *dunce* has been conjoined to words like *fool*, *stupid*, *idiot*, *dullard*, and *dolt* for time immemorial.

Rule #1 of the social classroom states, "Don't be the dunce!" It's a simple rule and one that the typical student is able to grasp without much arm-twisting. For the consequences of ignoring its valuable lesson is an embarrassment and humiliation too much for most dignified souls to endure.

Ironically, this very unattractive and shame-laden word *dunce* was derived from an intriguing Scotsman who lived back in the late thirteenth, early fourteenth century. His name was Jon Duns (often known in history as Duns Scotus). And if you pronounce his surname, Duns, properly, you would find that it sounds just like our word *dunce*. That's because it *is* the same word. Jon Duns Scotus has been inextricably tied to the idea of recalcitrant, shame-faced idiocy for hundreds of years.

I run a Bible college called Ellerslie. Interestingly, Ellerslie is a Scottish name. It's named after the birthplace of another notable Scot: William Wallace. These two men, Wallace and Duns, were born a mere four years apart and twenty miles away from each other. So it seems that whether I want it or not, being named Ellerslie brings me uncomfortably close to the front door of another Scot with a less attractive name. As a result, I feel somewhat of a providential kinship with this unfortunate "dunce" from seven hundred years ago.

Though Duns's name is forever tied to the idea of the thickskulled dolt, history attests to the fact that Jon Duns was actually a brilliant man. In fact, the word *brilliant* would be a vast understatement. Many in his generation considered him the world's most intelligent man while he was alive, and many scholars throughout history would attest to the fact that he was likely one of the most astute and developed minds throughout the entire thousand year epoch known to us as the Middle Ages.

This begs an important and obvious question. How did a man noted for such brilliance go down in history as such an imbecile? The answer to that question is extremely important to this book.

The recasting of Jon Duns as an "imbecilic dolt" didn't happen overnight. It happened over centuries. In fact, it was well over two hundred years after Duns's death that his followers, The Dunces, came under critical scrutiny.

Duns, a Franciscan Theologian, though brilliant, held to a rather simple view of the universe. He believed that all things centered upon the Person of Jesus Christ. He believed that since the entire universe was built by Christ, one could only properly understand it through the interpretive hermeneutic tool of the Person of Jesus Christ and by means of His Divine Revelation, the Holy Scriptures.

Duns Scotus actually did wear a pointy hat. And so did his followers, the Dunces. But the pointed hat — or dunce cap — meant something very different then than it does today. The hat pointed like a decided finger towards Heaven, declaring the One through whom all true knowledge and understanding is gained and approved. It was a symbol of the centrality of Jesus Christ in everything.

For two hundred and fifty years after the passing of Duns Scotus, history and western culture had moved forward with only deep appreciation for the contributions of Duns Scotus. But, in the sixteenth and seventeenth centuries something happened that changed everything.

The Renaissance brought a frontal assault on Duns's reasonings, and therefore on all his followers.

What was most shocking is that the leaders of the Renaissance brought serious allegations not just against the Dunces, but against God. They accused God of withholding knowledge from His Creation and refusing humankind access to the true potential of science and reasoning. They declared Him an oppressor of the masses — an obstacle to knowledge that must be rejected and moved out of the way.

And so, in light of these shocking charges against God, Humanism snubbed its nose at Duns's teachings on the "primacy of Christ," impeaching Jesus and officially removing Him from the Chancellor office over human education and reason — a position which He had held for over a thousand years in the Western world. This unthinkable step was greeted with hearty support all throughout the scholarly corridors in Western Europe, causing the new slogan of education to be (and I paraphrase for the sake of making a point): "Don't be a Dunce! Believe in the innate power of Man!"

The pressure was on. The educated world was swayed by this attractive new way of thinking. They began abandoning their old religious moorings in favor of this innovative "man-centered" ideology.

In the 16th century, a legion of faithful Dunces — those who believed in the primacy of Christ — took their stand against this erosion of Truth. The Dunces stood resolutely against this new wave of Renaissance thinking as if defending the Gospel itself.

History attests to how they were treated. These Dunces became synonymous with recalcitrant, incorrigible idiocy. They were stuck in the corner of intellectual society and deemed inferior. Their ideas were considered yesterday's ideas. The world was moving forward, and those that would dare attempt to stop its forward revolution would be caught beneath the chariot wheels.

• • • • •

To the true Church, "idiocy" has always been fashionable. Paul was willing to appear an idiot, a fool, and weakling in order for the strength of the Gospel of Jesus Christ to be clearly enunciated in his generation and throughout the world. Even Jesus Christ Himself was labeled out of His mind, and He never flinched or reacted in His own defense.

But we of the sacred mind are easily pulled away by the allurement of human vanity.

Let's be honest. If we had a choice, we prefer to appear smart rather than dumb, lucid rather than idiotic, and scholarly rather than scattered.

Ego looms in our souls like a floating metallic substance. The enemy malevolently draws this "ego" to the surface, using the magnet of social pressure and the irresistible pull of public acceptance and esteem. "You can be seen as intelligent! You can impress everyone with your amazing knowledge and insight. There is just *one thing* you need to do…"

That "one thing" has drawn many a sincere follower of Christ into the clutches of the avant-garde intellectuals of the day.

That's why I think it's high time we as Christians remember our heritage and the words of our Master. He forewarned us that the path of obedience is also the way of suffering. He told us ahead of time in no uncertain terms that to follow Him and make Him our center of learning and life would cause us to be deemed the offscouring of the world.

I propose we stop evaluating the Dunce cap based on what "they" will say about it, but only based on what God says about it.

I respect Jon Duns Scotus. That by no means should be interpreted as a statement of unanimity with his every teaching. Duns was of Catholic descent, and I am definitely not of the same heritage in that regard — seeing that I come from seven generations of Protestant/Evangelical pastors.

But Duns Scotus and I wear the same pointy hat. I, like him and his Dunces, believe that my mind, to be truly refined and cultivated, must find its source of reason, knowledge, and understanding in the Person of Jesus Christ and in the revelation of Jesus Christ (known as the Holy Scriptures).

If that position makes me a Dunce, then I will gladly wear the hat of infamy alongside my Scottish neighbor named Jon.

The reason I am highlighting Duns Scotus in the beginning of this book is to clarify something very important. This is a book about educational training — a very specific type of education training. It's not the liberal arts form of education so familiar to us these days, but something far more poignant and significant. This is a book that intends to articulate what makes this particular training school named Ellerslie different and necessary in our modern day. We are seeking to bring back the kind of Christ-central education that forces the words *dunce, dodo, dullard, dolt,* and *dumbbell* back into the vernacular of the modern world.

In other words, we aren't pandering after the approval of the masses. In fact, we fully expect their scorn and rejection.

Ellerslie is a "college" of the old school Christianity. We are interested in building men and women who boldly believe the Scriptures and are unashamed of their faith. We are eager to see men and women who know how to put Jesus Christ back into His proper position, and thus return to the intellectual strength that comes from embracing the Creator's mind, thoughts, and reasoning toward His Creation.

The accusations today are the same as during the Renaissance. Modern humanists believe that to reason outward from Christ Jesus and from the Scriptures is to repress true intelligence. It is deemed boorish and anti-intellectual by the high-minded.

But we affirm that Christ-centeredness is the basis of true intelligence and healthy reason.

We believe that the true roots of all academic study is found first and foremost in the Word of God. God invented mathematics, science, theology, language, and literature. He says, "Come, let us reason together" (Isaiah 1:18). God Himself sets forth the model and the character of the premier student — empowering His followers towards love, diligence, excellence, peace, patience, mercy, kindness, generosity, and justice. It is in God's Word that we learn how to rightly divide truth and how to avoid the bait of the evil that seeks to undermine and ruin our souls.

We believe it is time for the bold return of the Dunces — men and women who do not fear the scorn of the "intellectually elite" or kowtow to the mockery of the academic guild. In Christ's day, the intellectual elite crowd fashioned a cross and pinned Him ruthlessly to it. During the Renaissance, they fashioned a paper cone shaped hat and mockingly scrawled the word "Dunce" on it.

In our day, the cultural penalty for "intellectual incorrigibility" may look different. But it will certainly come from those very same ancient spirits that seek to exalt man's thinking above the thinking of Jesus Christ, the Creator of all.

The Serpent has been in the same business from the beginning. His name is Lucifer, which in the Hebrew means "the bringer of light." He boasts of a knowledge that exalts man and disposes of God. He is the purveyor of this pablum. When all is said and done, it is he whom we oppose.

Just like in the Garden, Lucifer brings "hidden knowledge" — knowledge he claims God doesn't want us to have. His agenda is to cause us to turn a jaundiced eye towards the One who is known as the Truth. Throughout history, this subtle Serpent has created wave after wave of "enlightenment" to sway those vulnerable towards the fruit of hidden knowledge that dangles from the tree.

Today, we are in the midst of a new wave of enlightenment. Lucifer is on the move again. And this wave of new knowledge (which is nothing more than ancient lies repackaged into modern vernacular) is flooding into this country at breakneck speed even as I write this paragraph. And it would appear that those who would dare oppose his agenda with their antiquated ideas are going to find themselves wearing pointy hats and sitting in the proverbial corner of the intellectual classroom.

Just like a physical battle, the war of ideas offers two clear options to those of us wearing pointy dunce hats.

The first is to surrender to the "overpowering ideology" and negotiate terms of peace with it.

The second is to keep swinging your sword until you either win or you die trying.

Ellerslie has sided unequivocally with Wallace and Duns. The battle is on. We choose option two.

II.

PICKING UP WHERE HARVARD LEFT OFF

My uncle George took me to visit Harvard University when I was thirteen. Dressed awkwardly in a suit coat and tie, I strolled the grounds of the venerable school with my mouth ajar, trying to take it all in.

My uncle was making his pitch for me to pursue an Ivy League future. Uncle George was himself an alumni of both Harvard and Yale, for his undergraduate and graduate studies respectively. He strongly urged me to set my sights on either of these two schools, but did add that he would still bestow his magnanimous approval upon me if I were to select either Princeton or the University of Virginia as alternatives.

But when I graduated from high school, I sorely disappointed my well-meaning, intellectually elite uncle. Even after all those impressive tours of ivy-league beauty and grandeur, I chose to go west instead of east, where the IQs were lower and so were the graduation requirements. After I graduated from college with an unremarkable mixture of Whitworth College and Colorado Christian University, Uncle George became rather quiet. He'd spent a lot of time and money planting the vision for my heady excellence, but to no avail.

I felt kind of bad, for his sake, that I turned out more salt-of-the-earth than Ivy-League-ish in my academic prowess. But all was not lost.

My Uncle George (who has since passed on) might be proud to hear that I've finally caught the Harvard vision after all. It turns out that I'm actually quite a nice fit for this venerable institution. In a dumbed-down, colloquial sort-of-way, Harvard and I are bosom friends, or, as Anne Shirley would say it, "kindred spirits."

Just picture it…

Eric Ludy — the loud-mouthed defender of conservative Biblical thinking and Christ-centered living — goes prancing off into the sunset, linking arms with Harvard University — the brash purveyor of high-minded, liberal, Marxist, communist, and socialist pablum that is currently flooding into American society.

Hmmm. Something doesn't seem right about that picture.

Oh, maybe I forgot to clarify this earlier, but when I say that I've finally caught the vision for Harvard, I mean the "old" Harvard. The Harvard from back in the mid 1600's.

Back in 1646, while defining the "laws, liberties, and orders" for their training, Harvard declared to its students, "Every one shall consider the main End of his life and studies, to know God and Jesus Christ which is Eternal life. John xvii.3."[2]

But through the years, something went haywire at

---

2   Laws, Liberties, and Orders of Harvard College, circa 1646

Harvard. With all those high IQs mingling together, there must have been some kind of chemical reaction that took place. Somewhere along the line, they decided that, instead of seeking to know God more, they would be a lot better off rejecting Him altogether.

Harvard started out understanding that the entire purpose of education is to showcase the Person of Jesus Christ. Their college motto was *Veritas Christo et Ecclesiae*, meaning "Truth for Christ and the Church." Their goal was to build Christian ministers that would carry the light of God's Truth into this country. And now, shockingly, Harvard is the leader in producing those most adept at stamping it out. Talk about veering off from your original charter.

Here's the irony. Everyone nowadays perceives the Harvard graduate to be the epitome of intellectual excellence. And yet, Harvard started out as the school of Dunces. It was their great ideal at Harvard to "Lay Christ in the bottom, as the only foundation of all sound knowledge and learning." And they added to this conviction a very reasonable observation and conclusion: "And seeing the Lord only giveth wisdom, let every one seriously set himself by prayer in secret to seek it of Him (Prov. II.3)."[3]

This Harvardian dictate was the precise conclusion of Jon Duns Scotus. This concept of the "primacy of Christ" was the same idea that caused the name "Duns" to be inextricably tied to the notion of stupidity. Harvard started out with the clear objective of building "Dunces" for Christ.

And it wasn't just Harvard that set out to do this.

---

3   Rule number two in Harvard's Rules and Precepts, 1646

Princeton, Yale, Dartmouth, Duke, Northwestern, Southern California, Vanderbilt, Syracuse and a shocking number of other well-respected universities originally set out to defy the notions of European humanism, by putting Christ back into His rightful place.

In the early days of Harvard, America was laboring hard to return to the foundations of true knowledge and understanding — to gain back sanity in the realm of education. And how did they believe it should be done? By once again establishing education on the moorings of Jesus Christ and the Revelation of Scripture.

So, what happened to the Harvard Dunces?

Well, it's a long story. But, it can be summarized in one simple idea: the battering ram of Lucifer never sleeps. Those that close their eyes to it, for even one hour, are sure to have their gates lost to the onslaught of his evil agenda.

III.

THE POWER OF "THEY"

It was a tree that led to the fall of man. And, ironically, it was a tree that led to the salvation of man. Two trees, two outcomes.

The same two trees still stand before each of us today.

The first is the bait for carnal knowledge, while the second is the call to come and allow the carnal man to die at the Cross of Christ. Ironically, both trees lead to a death. The first, to eternal death and separation from God, while the second leads to the death of that which stands in the way of you and eternal life.

The name of the tree in the midst of the garden that the Serpent was craftily bating Eve to eat from was "The Tree of the Knowledge of Good and Evil." The Serpent accused God of keeping His creation from this tasty treat. He indicted God with oppressively controlling His people, repressing their full potential, and unduly keeping them from knowledge that would empower them to be as God is.

This lie is at the root of every single "enlightenment" that storms the coastlines of culture with its waves of intellectualism. Every enlightenment is a call to throw off the restraints of God-oppression and to think without the God mind-cuffs wrapped around the wrists of our every thought.

But although God has been accused in every generation of stultifying intellectual progress, the accusation is baseless and false. In actuality, it is wholly opposite the truth. Like declaring tooth brushing as the great enemy of healthy teeth, it is a lie that, if heeded, leads to serious cavities.

God is not against the intellectual development of His creation. But, as a good father, He knows that certain knowledge will only cause harm if it is given prematurely.

As a father, I understand this. For instance, it is because I love my three-year-old son that I tell him to stay away from the gas stove in the kitchen. This by no means should indicate to my little munchkin that the knowledge of the gas stove and how to work it is in itself wrong, but merely that such knowledge absent the requisite maturity to properly appropriate it would lead to a house on fire.

In fact, I intend to teach my three-year-old how to use the stove in due time. And I will teach him this knowledge because I love him and because I want him to function up to the full potential and strength he was created to exhibit.

Isn't it also reasonable that God is the same? He knows that without maturity, knowledge can lead to all forms of evil. For instance, knowledge of how to build an explosive in the hands of a rebellious teenager with a vendetta against his school can become a recipe for injury or death. But the knowledge of how to build an explosive in the hands of a mature adult can lead to the creation of the combustion engine, and thusly the train, the automobile, the plane, and a million other helpful tools.

Enlightenment has one intent: to turn children against their fathers. It seeks to root out any and all authority. And it does this by sneaking into households and talking to the kids. It asks the question,

> *Does your father let you experience the joys of lighting the gas stove?*

The child turns toward the Serpent and answers back,

> *Why, no. I am not yet old enough to handle the gas stove. My father says that it would hurt me.*

The Serpent then appears shocked and dismayed, and with a comforting voice says,

> *I don't wish to speak ill of your father, but that is simply not true, my son. For your father knows that if you used the stove, as he must know you could, you would have endless supplies of hash brown, eggs, waffles, pancakes, and all other manner of tasty foods whenever your heart desired them.*

The child, a bit confused, answers back,

> *But, you aren't suggesting my father is lying to me, are you?*

The Serpent puts his arm around the shoulder of the young lad and softly says,

> *I don't presume to know the motivation of your father, dear lad; I only know what is true. And that is you are perfectly capable of handling the gas stove without*

fear of harm. In fact, you are able to do far more than you probably realize. And it would appear your father has been purposely misleading you in order that he might keep you unduly and unfairly under his thumb of control.

The young child looks toward the floor and considers this revelation. The ramifications of these ideas are far reaching. If they were true, then how could he trust his father's word anymore? If what the Serpent was saying was true, then everything his father had ever told him would need to fall under scrutiny.

And this is the moment that the Serpent leans in and drives his argument home.

Little one, I know these things are hard to hear. But the strongest kids on your block have been using the gas stove for years now. And, as you well know, they are happy and healthy. In fact, I heard them discussing you the other day, wondering why you were so small and undernourished. They wondered if you had fallen for the age-old lie of the fathers. And it appears you have. For the stupid and gullible ones are often easy to recognize. They are the ones unenlightened. They consider grabbing the knob of the gas stove a "sin," when in actuality it is only an act of virtuous advancement and growth of the human spirit.

There is something pricked inside the young lad at this particular speech by the Serpent that causes our previously innocent little child to rise up and grab the gas stove. There is something in him that pricks him even as he does it. The "father-consciousness" is still there, but this time he ignores it, for the jocular jeering voices of the other kids on the block are too much for our little example child to withstand.

The devil is an expert at this game. He has made it his business for near six thousand years since the Garden to question the integrity of God's manner of instruction.

As I see it, there are two ways of responding to this supposed enlightenment as Christians. The first option is what Adam chose to do. He listened to Eve's appeal. As the juice of the freshly eaten fruit dribbled down her beautiful chin and the grand vision of liberty and freedom exulted within her now-awakened mind, she turned towards her husband and sought to have him join her in this powerful realization of personal power and autonomy from the oppressive "Father-instruction." This Adam did, to his ruin and that of his descendants.

The second option is to listen to God's answer. When Eve comes bearing the freshly picked fruit of Sozzini, Kant, Darwin, Freud, or Marx, Adam should turn to God and lay the Serpent's accusations before Him and let Him reply.

The first Adam failed. Jesus is known as the Last Adam, the Second Man. He is the One that responded properly to the failure of His Bride. Adam should have come to the Throne of Grace and sought mercy. God may have said, "Adam, I told you that the day in which the fruit was eaten there would be death." And Adam may have replied, "I understand, God. But is there any other way than for Eve to die for heeding the ideology of the Serpent and eating the forbidden fruit?" I imagine God in such a circumstance bending low and looking deeply into Adam's eyes and saying, "Why yes, Adam. You could die for her."

Jesus has done the work to turn this tide of Serpentine duping. But the Spirit of the Last Adam who laid down His life for His Bride must enter into us as His children — that we might be willing to follow in His footsteps and suffer to see other fruit-eaters set free from the Satanic spell.

But we also must realize that this spell is a strong one. So strong, in fact, that the very life of God's Son, Jesus, was sacrificed in order to redeem us from its evil effects. So, as we go into this world to fight against these lies, we must understand the gravity and seriousness of this battle.

This is primarily an issue of pride.

Satan's downfall was pride. And so is ours.

It says of Lucifer that he "corrupted [his] wisdom for the sake of [his] splendor" (Ezekiel 28:17) and that he "desired to rise above God and ascend above the stars."

Harvard University started out with such a lovely and virtuous purpose, fashioned out of the side of Christ, to be His helper in His grand redemptive purposes on this earth. But, just like Eve, Harvard was beguiled from the singularity of focus that is in Christ (2 Corinthians 11:3).

But this isn't just Harvard's story. This is the story of an ever growing number of Christian enterprises. All of which started with a charter to honor the Word of Christ, but that found themselves decades later defying the very God who gave them birth.

"[Lucifer] corrupted [his] wisdom for the sake of [his] splendor" (Ezekiel 28:17).

The same could be said of Harvard. For the sake of their own splendor — their own intellectual credibility — they corrupted their wisdom. The same could be said of Princeton and Yale. In desiring to gain the approval of the intellectual elite, they followed the path of the Serpent, and traded out intimacy with God for the approval of the enlightened kids on the block.

The Serpent arrived on Harvard's campus in the 1700's. The next wave of "enlightenment" was upon the world and its wave, this time, struck the shores of North America.

The message of the enlightenment was clear. Immanuel Kant, one of the premier voices within this wave, spoke of the glittering brilliance of the enlightenment as a passionate preacher might speak of the Gospel of Jesus Christ. But Kant's "gospel" was not the good news of being freed from the shackles of sin and its subsequent penalty, but rather it was a message of being freed from the shackles of "God." The diabolical notion was that humankind had been under the thumb of the Bible and under the dogmatism of this narrow lens of reasoning for far too long, but now, by eating the fruit of the Serpent's bidding, we, the human race, could be finally free to use our own intellectual capacities in determining what to believe and how to act.

The enlightenment defied the Bible. It defied Jesus Christ. But, as many Harvardians reasoned, it also had some grand and noble ideas woven into its framework. After all, it promoted ideas that were congruent with the Biblical ideal — ideas like equality for all, liberty, and justice for the people. And it didn't outright say that God and the Bible were wrong — it merely sought to reason independently from it in order to be truly "honest and fair" in its assessment of things, letting science be the final vote on what is true and what is not.

It was fruit hanging from the tree, poking at the intellectual pride of the scholar, asking him to join the brightest minds in the world in thinking and reasoning with "fairness and honesty" instead of under the "dogmatism" of one singular lens.

It also pressed one additional thought into those already predisposed to fall for the bait of intellectual esteem. It made up a dunce cap, set a chair in the corner of the room of all the brightest minds, and said, "We know that you, like us, are truly intellectual and scholarly, and that you too will see it the way we see it. After all, you don't want to wear this cone-shaped, idiot's hat, do you?"

The Harvard tale of Biblical disavowal and ultimately their choice to disregard and directly oppose the very charter that started their school is deeply disturbing to me as a Christian leader in our modern day. But it has shown me something very important. Though you may start out strong, it is very possible to end quite wrong.

I may be a few hundred years late. But I want to return to the School of the Dunces. I want to build a school that will defy the Kants and laugh at Lucifer's fruit. I want to see young minds trained *not* to esteem the opinion of the academic guild over the opinion of the Word of God.

Such a venture, I realize, sounds a bit like a trip into the ISIS war room to ask them to all bend their knees to the Lordship of Jesus Christ. But what's life without a grand vision?

I say let's fight to see true intelligence once again reign in the hearts and minds of men. By that I don't mean to throw out science and reason, but to immolate them into the understanding and comprehension of something greater, or should I say *Someone* greater — the Someone that created all knowledge, all truth, all things in the first place.

My Uncle George may not have meant for me to interpret all his Harvardian overtures in the way I have. But I hope he sees, even from the other side of the eternal veil, that I am indeed carrying the banner of his alma-mater. At least the version of it that should be carried by every Christian.

IV.

THE TRIUMVIRATE OF TRUE EDUCATION

... Guard what has been entrusted to you, avoiding worldly and empty chatter and the opposing arguments of what is falsely called "knowledge."

1 Timothy 6:20

There is something notable about doing something novel and new. But such notoriety would be misplaced here in Windsor, Colorado. What Ellerslie is doing has been done before — in fact, many times over. We are doing something rather old-fashioned at our campus here in Windsor, Colorado. We are training Dunces — men and women educated to think and reason from the center-point of the Word of God in Text, Person, and Action.

Ellerslie is merely picking up the assignment that Harvard, Yale, and Princeton abandoned. We are seeking to reestablish the triumvirate expression of the Word God as the headwaters of our students' education.

1. The Word of God in Text – **The Scriptures**
2. The Word of God in Person – **Jesus Christ**
3. The Word of God in Action – **The Cross**

It might sound strange, but as an educational institution our primary agenda is not the impartation of mere knowledge. It is the impartation of real Life. We don't want our students to leave our campus merely smarter; we want them to leave changed. We want them to be spiritually quickened, morally strengthened, practically skilled, and intellectually centered.

When Harvard began, it was established in the safe confines of a land "apart" and one in which its Christ-centered ideology was applauded and kept sacrosanct. Early America was the ideal soil for the establishment of such an institution. Today, the cultural atmosphere that Ellerslie faces is quite different. The spiritual environment of our culture is hostile to the Dunce. It's like attempting to teach a class on the primacy of Christ in a classroom in which Sozzini, Kant, Darwin, Freud, and Marx all hold lectures simultaneously.

Call me old-fashioned, but truth is truth. And no matter the discoveries of these supposed intellectuals, I agree with Christ in that it is only "truth that sets free."

George Orwell postulated a world in which "love" would be twisted to mean "hate" and "peace" would be convoluted to mean "war." In our world, "true intelligence" has been twisted to mean "Dunce" and "true idiocy" has been paraded about as if it were in fact "brilliance."

We have emptied education of Christ. And without Christ we have lost the Creator of all things.

Imagine trying to describe the formation of Microsoft

while trying to hide the existence of Bill Gates. Or how about attempting to explain the origins of the lightbulb minus the life of Edison, the game of basketball without Naismith, or the ceiling of the Sistine Chapel after deleting Michelangelo from the history books? Such learning is not high and lofty, but low and ignorant.

Mommy, the Emperor known as Education is naked. He is missing the most important thing in his clothing ensemble — the clothes themselves.

To remove Jesus from the center of education is the equivalent of removing hydrogen and oxygen from H20. You can call what you have left "water" but it's really only a little "2" with absolutely zero capacity to slack your thirst. Try drinking it and you will certainly see.

It's not just the secular universities that have walked headlong into this grand parade of nakedness, but even many modern Christian educational institutions have begun to be swallowed up in the ruse.

Some have begun to teach evolution, some have denied the premise that Jesus is the Way, the Truth, and the Life — the only way to the Father. Some have left the moorings of the text of Scripture as their basis of reasoning and have considered their own intellect worthy of supplying a lasting foundation able to withstand winds and rains.

The wooing of the Serpent is strong, his spell powerful. He offers worldly pleasures and accouterments to those who will heed his syrupy counsel.

At Ellerslie we boldly believe that the Bible is, in fact, in Truth, and, indeed, the Word of God captured in textual form. And we have built our entire training around that belief.

We believe that in recruiting the Bible as our lead professor, and the Holy Spirit as its chief spokesman, that we have, in doing so, gained the greatest teaching staff on earth.

Little kids on the playground might say, "My dad can beat up your dad!" But at Ellerslie we are bit more mature in our bragging. We say, "Harvard, Yale, Stanford, and Princeton, our teachers are smarter than your teachers!"

It's quite a special thing, indeed, to know that God Himself is the One doing the teaching on our campus.

V.

THE TWENTY-SIX LEAD SOLDIERS

Karl Marx once stated:

> *Give me twenty-six lead soldiers and I will change the world.*

Those ominous words of Karl Marx still stand today as a haunting testimony to the power of written communication. Twenty-six lead soldiers to Marx were the twenty-six letters on a typewriter or printing press. And Marx proved correct. He did change the world with those twenty-six soldiers. However, he didn't change it for the better.

Though Marx may have coined the phrase "twenty-six lead soldiers," Marx was certainly not the first to realize the history-shaping power of the alphabet and the written word.

In the fourteenth century B.C., God, with His own almighty finger, wrote, using the letters, words, and grammatical sentence structure of men, on tablets of stone. And then after God communed with Moses on

Mount Sinai for forty days, He said to Moses, "Write these things down for a memorial in a book."

It was God who began the notion of changing the world through the "Twenty-Six Soldiers."[4] But, like everything that God begins that is "good — very good," the Serpent seeks to disturb it and distort its purity.

God established the basis of all true education as Himself. And it is the Bible that captures this basis of all true education and introduces us to the One known as the Eternal, Immutable, Omniscient, Almighty Creator of the heavens and the earth. The Bible, in a sense, is really just Heaven fleshed out in earthly letters, sounds, words, phrases, sentences, paragraphs, chapters, and books. It's the Almighty condescending to make Himself known to lowly man — the Creator stooping low to express His love, mercy, kindness, and grace to an undeserving people.

He's saying, "If you want to understand why you are here and what you are supposed to do with the life you have been given, I will tell you."

The sixty-six books of the Bible are such an extraordinary and other-worldly heavenly enunciation. It is the literal textbook of life, the map to buried treasure, the instruction manual to knowing God, the unhindered access into the Creator's mind to understand all things.

The Bible is supernatural in its origins and in its content. And any serious student of its text must acknowledge that in studying it, they are encountering something far greater than human literature, and, in fact, are running headlong into living words given by God Himself. And these words

---

4   The Hebrew language technically only has twenty-two letters, but hopefully the concept I'm purporting is caught and understood.

all point to one singular Man and one singular Action. And this one singular Man, known as Jesus Christ, and this one singular Action, known as the Cross, is heralded, even inside this very Book of books, as the centerpiece of all reasoning, knowledge, and understanding.

It's not just a singular brilliant man named Duns who believed this, lived this, and proclaimed this. Men and women throughout the ages have also willingly yielded their brow to this dunce cap.

Many of the highest intelligent quotients in history centered their education and life pursuits around the Word of God in Text, Person, and Action. For instance, Bacon, Mendel, Planck, Kepler, Newton, Copernicus, Galileo, Pascal, and Faraday all held to the centrality of the Word of God in their thinking, reasoning, and discovery. Many of the greatest inventors in history, such as Pasteur, Carver, Fleming, Kelvin, Gutenberg, held to the same. Even Bach, one of the world's greatest composers, considered his prime motivation the glory and knowledge of Jesus Christ. While many of the greatest world leaders like Wilberforce, Washington, Lincoln, and Churchill viewed the Word of God as God's revealed Truth, and the requisite centerpiece for the proper ruling of nations.

Early protestant America defied the enlightenment and the brush fire of humanism that was sweeping the European world. They proudly wore their Dunce caps and labored to bring the Person of Jesus Christ back to the world that was quickly losing Him. They intended to do this through education. And they shared Daniel Webster's opinion on the subject, who said "Education is useless without the Bible."

At Ellerslie, we believe the same.

In Guttenberg's, Wycliffe's, and Tyndale's day, twenty-six lead soldiers changed the face of Europe, inspiring true education to sweep the land, because the Bible was made available to common men and women.

May God's Twenty-Six Lead Soldiers, known as the Holy Scriptures, once again bring about such a revival in our land.

VI.

BEWARE THE ARYAN PARAGRAPH

When Hitler was taking power in Germany, he did a lot of wonderful things. In fact, in many ways, he was a savior of the German people, revolutionizing their society both fiscally and practically. If Hitler had died near the inception of his role as chancellor of Germany, he may have gone down in history alongside the likes of Ghandi, Mandela, and Martin Luther King Jr.

But there was darkness to Hitler that wasn't readily apparent to the casual onlooker.

Every broken dam starts with a small crack. If the crack is not properly tended, it eventually grows into a bigger one. The rule of "the crack in the dam" is simple. If you shrug your shoulders at a small crack, soon everything that took so long to build will be washed away in the flood of dissipation.

Hitler made a crack in the dam of the German church. It didn't seem that big. In fact, it was so small that it almost seemed invisible. This was, in part, due to the fact that the German church was deliberately closing their eyes whenever they looked in the direction of the crack.

It might sound strange that the German church stood alongside Adolph Hitler in his extermination of the Jews. But they did. Or maybe it would best be stated that the German church didn't stand against Adolf Hitler in his extermination of the Jews. They shrugged their shoulders at the crack in the dam and soon they were swimming in the morass of his moral turpitude.

History refers to this "crack in the dam" as the Aryan Paragraph. Woven into the fabric of all of Hitler's wonderful ideology, fiscally responsible methods, and Christian-sensitive political notions, there was one small fly in the ointment. And this fly wasn't even that big. It was just a singular paragraph of text.

But this paragraph of text separated out the Aryans from the non-Aryans. Or, as history would best say it, "The non-Jews from the Jews." It gave special rights to the white German non-Jews, and removed rights from those of Jewish descent.

At first it was subtle and almost nondescript. It wasn't enough to make a fuss over. But it was a crack. It was a direct violation against the nature of Jesus Christ who shows favoritism to no man and treats all as equals before the Cross.

The German church chose to shrug their shoulders at the Aryan paragraph. After all, their nation was stronger than it had ever been, finances and provision for the church in Germany was burgeoning, and to stand against Hitler on this little point just didn't seem like the wisest thing to do. After all, Hitler was doing so many good things for the German church, so to complain may seem like staring a gift horse in the mouth.

But that one small paragraph was the crack that led to the breaking of the dam. The German church became complicit in the extermination of millions of Jews, simply because of their silence.

Martin Luther said, "If I profess with loudest voice and clearest exposition every portion of the truth of God except that little point which the world and the devil are at that moment attacking, I am not confessing Christ, however boldly I may be professing Christ. Where the battle rages, there the loyalty of the soldier is proved, and to be steady on all the battlefield besides, is mere flight and disgrace if he flinches at that point."

The Aryan Paragraph is in one form or another injected into every generation. And in every generation this paragraph always seems so small and such a tremendous bother to address. Or at least the devil begs you to see it that way. And in every generation there are certain things that society will declare as officially off-limits for the Church to speak about. These are topics or social ideas that are to be left alone by the Christians. And if the Christians fall in line with this social expectation, then Christianity can go on unmolested by the government. Even in the most extreme communist countries that has been proven true.

And that is why in every generation there are always two churches. There is the church that panders after position, plaudits, and worldly accouterments. And even the most wicked governments have honored and prospered the advancement of such churches. And then there is the church that stands up against the Aryan

Paragraph and declares it wrong. And in most countries today, where Christianity is persecuted, this church is known as the "Underground Church" — or, as history would attest, the "True Church."

Deitrich Boenhoeffer, as a Christian leader in Germany in the days of Adolph Hitler, chose to stand apart from the German Christianity of his day. He stood against the Aryan paragraph. And he was killed for it.

In every hour, there is an easy path and a narrow path — there is a way of convenience (which demands compromise) and a way of obedience (which demands a stand against the Aryan Paragraph).

Many leaders in higher education believe that to walk in agreement with government is the lone means of survival for the state of education. Such compromise makes sense, if the end goal of education is to prepare students to be made likened unto current society rather than to be made likened unto the Person of Jesus Christ. And such compromise also makes sense if the financial endowment of the institution takes precedence over the truthfulness of the institution. An institution built to train Dunces cannot — no matter the pressure, no matter the threats, no matter the consequence — allow the injection of an Aryan Paragraph into its charter, into its curriculum, or into its training.

Those which desire to train the true church must function as the true church in the moments when such definition is most imperative.

Ellerslie is willing to become a training program for the underground church. We desire our students to learn to live like Boenhoeffer, to suffer like Wurmbrand, to preach like Spurgeon, and to die as Elliot. We do not train our students to overlook the Aryan Paragraph, but rather, to recognize it, expose it, and oppose it.

We have a passion for the bold return of the Dunces. Another way of saying that is the bold return of those that will not accept the Aryan Paragraph sitting down.

When Christ draws His sword, His Church draws the sword.

VII.

THE BARMEN FELLOWSHIP

Admittedly, Ellerslie is an odd place. Or I should say it's an odd place for those who are used to the feel, the vibe, and the atmosphere of the world. Whereas "odd" is not usually a compliment, I utilize it here with the utmost respect to our school. For Ellerslie is an "otherly" environment — a little taste of heaven in a world so lacking that heavenly shimmer. It's a place purposely built for students to spend a season focused solely on One Thing. And that One Thing is Jesus Christ and the amazing work He accomplished at the Cross!

For those who want to fit into the world, be popular, and strategically avoid Dunce caps, there are many other options for Biblical training. If "cool" is your motto, then we would strongly encourage you to look elsewhere for your discipleship. We specialize here in Windsor, Colorado, in working with those who are desirous to really live out audaciously bold and love-infused Christianity. If you want a growl in your faith, a fire in your witness, and a shout of triumph in your soul, Ellerslie may be a great fit. But, if it's hip, avant-garde Christianity you are drawn to . . . please, please consider other options.

In May of 1934, a group of protestant German pastors gathered together in Barmen, Germany. Undoubtedly, this little gathering could have been termed, "The Bold Return of the Dunces." In a country that was decidedly Protestant Christian (can you say 70%?), it might have seemed strange that these conservative, kind, loving Protestant pastors were deemed the "crazies," the "wild-eyed," and the "rabble-rousers" — but these German pastors had all willingly chosen to place proverbial Dunce caps on their heads and travel to Barmen. They all agreed that, as God-fearing, Bible-reverencing, and Christ-centered leaders, they couldn't stand by and be silent while Hitler destroyed the Jewish people.

There were 45 million Protestant Christians in Nazi Germany in 1934. And yet these bold men represented a group of only 150,000 Christian men and women that were willing to "count the cost and speak out." Shockingly, only three out of every one thousand Christians were willing to rise up and say something. Nine-hundred ninety-seven out of every one thousand Christians in 1934 Germany stood by and silently acquiesced to Hitler's extermination of the Jews.

And so, after three days of conferring and ratifying their stance, together these men signed the Barmen Declaration and became known from that time forward as "The Confessing Church." They counted the cost. They knew it meant standing against the political and cultural tide of Nazism. But they did it anyway. They did it because they were sheep and not goats, wheat and not tares. They were "Christian" Christians.

Ellerslie wants to be a Barmen-like destination here in America — a rallying place for all those that can't sit by and do nothing. Though our knees may knock, we want to be counted amongst the three and not counted amongst the nine-hundred ninety-seven.

The year was 478 B.C. The life of the Jewish nation hung in the balance, facing sure extinction in the upcoming days unless God intervened and did something miraculous. It was in this context that wise uncle Mordecai spoke, in all seriousness, to his niece Esther. And as I repeat Modecai's words, I want you to hear them as if they were words spoken directly to you and not to a Jewish girl near 2,500 years ago.

> *[Dear Christian], if you remain completely silent at this time, relief and deliverance will arise...from another place, but you and your father's house will perish. Yet who knows whether you have come to the kingdom for such a time as this?*

You are alive right now. You have reached a point of maturity where your decision of moral will can and must affect the world around you. You have a tongue. What are you doing with it? You have hands and feet. What are you doing with them? You have resources, talents, and abilities. What are you doing with them? If you remain silent at this time, God will certainly still bring about His ends, but who knows whether you have come to this time, place, and state of maturity and understanding for such a time as this? Who knows, but that you were crafted by God for such an hour?

If you would like to be strengthened to use your tongue, hands, feet, resources, talents, and abilities for the Kingdom of God and live out a bold version of the Christian faith, we are currently marching down Brickbat Lane here in Windsor, Colorado. We would love for you to prayerfully consider joining us in the refining fires of spiritual discipleship.

With King David we groan, "Help, Lord, for the godly man ceases! For the faithful disappear from among the sons of men" (Psalm 12:1).

And then with one voice, united in a common prayer, we, the remnant of our dear and precious Savior exclaim, "But, Lord, build Your witness once again in this earth. And use us as your living stones!"

SURVIVING EXTINCTION

In summary, Ellerslie is all about the Bold Return of the Dunces. There are a lot of words that could be strategically used to replace the word *dunce* in our purpose statement. *Dumbbell*, *dumdum*, *dolt*, and *doofus* would all be wonderful replacements. However, *dodo* is the most hilarious option, and it works well for a finishing thought to this book.

The dodo bird was discovered in 1598 on the island of Mauritius. One dodo was killed, cooked, and eaten. It was found to be "very good meat." So, with no instinct to fight and no capacity for self-protection, the dodo, when faced with this newfound predatorial threat, had no resistance. It could not survive long. It had no choice but to go extinct.

Sure enough. Sixty-four years after its discovery, not a single dodo bird was left on planet earth.

Contrast the dodo bird with the sheep and a unique contradistinction appears. Both animals are weak, dumb, and slow, and both have proven a palette-pleasing tasty treat. However, the dodo bird died off in sixty-four years, while the sheep somehow still endures even to this day.

In fact, belying its vulnerable state, the sheep has outlasted the likes of such grand creatures as the Siberian tiger, the Irish elk, the cave lion, and even tyrannosaurus rex.

What is its secret?

Well, that's simple. The sheep has a shepherd. And that fact alone sets it apart as an animal that will continue to thrive even when disease, famine, wolves, bears, and lions attack.

The fact that we as Christians are likened to sheep in the Bible mustn't go unnoticed in this discussion. For though we appear vulnerable, pathetically dumb (at times), and a surprisingly tasty morsel for all the salivating host of darkness, we are not alone. We rest beneath the shelter of the Most High.

Christianity today appears against the ropes. Some, in fact, are even claiming that it is down for the count.

Futurist Michael Spencer penned these words nearly a decade ago: "We are on the verge — within 10 years — of a major collapse of evangelical Christianity."

Spencer surmised that, "Millions of Evangelicals will quit. Thousands of ministries will end. Christian media will be reduced, if not eliminated. Many Christian schools will go into rapid decline."[5]

Spencer declared a time frame. He said within ten years. Whereas these past ten years haven't shown a strengthening of Christianity in the West, I would say that we as the evangelical Christians have proven

---

5 http://www.internetmonk.com/archive/my-prediction-the-coming-evangelical-collapse-1

surprisingly resilient nonetheless. For we haven't yet gone the way of the dodo.

In fact, Christianity has survived every attack in every generation. And it certainly will survive this present meltdown as well. Remember, we have a Shepherd.

But that said, we shouldn't pretend that everything is just fine.

The culture we all currently live in is akin to a big stew pot full of boiling beezlenut oil.[6] It's the perfect set-up for the demise of Christianity as we know it. And if you look at the menu, this generation is boasting a very tasty dish, known as "Fried Christian." Biblical truth has grown passé. The post-modernists have taken the helm of the Christian industry and hold the controls of both the publishing realms and the music industry. Meanwhile the pulpits of North American Christianity seem mostly held by the guardians of mushy thinking.

It's suddenly considered "extreme" to simply believe Jesus to be God in the Flesh. It's considered "ignorant" to hold the text of Scripture as if it is, in fact, the Word of God. And it is deemed "wild-eyed fancy" to claim Jesus Christ to be the only way to God the Father.

Something has gone awry when the most basic of basic beliefs in the corridors of Christianity are considered by the church today as bizarre and ignorant conclusions.

Our parents' generation grew up in Sunday school. The current generation is growing up in daycare. Where our parents began life with a firm hold on absolute truth, this current generation doesn't seem to have a firm grip on anything, outside of their iPhone.

---

6   *Though beezlenut oil is an invention of Dr. Seuss, I understand it is pretty dangerous stuff, designed to quell any and all voices that stand contrary to the democratic ruler of every society: Mr. Status-Quo.*

And this is precisely why when someone asks us, "Why are you building Ellerslie?" we look at the desperate need for real, radical, and revolutionary Christian living and, pointing at that immense void, say, "That's why!"

ABOUT THE AUTHOR

There were three things growing up that Eric Ludy declared he would never become: a teacher, a missionary, and a pastor. He became all three. In a vain attempt to gain some worldly credibility he also became a writer. But seventeen books later, it's ironically his book writing has led to more scorn than the other three combined. In other words, his strategy backfired big time. Ludy is the president of Ellerslie Mission Society, the teaching pastor at the Church at Ellerslie, and the lead instructor in the Ellerslie Discipleship Training. He is descended from seven generations of pastors, totally uncool, somewhat skinny, and in Japan supposedly his last names means "Nerd." But, that said, he is clothed in the shed blood of His beloved Savior; Leslie, his wife of twenty years, still laughs at his jokes; and his six kids think he is Superman (or at least Clark Kent). So, all is well with the author of this book. He calls Windsor, Colorado home, but longs for his real home in Heaven where being a "fool for Christ" finally will be realized to be the most brilliant life-decision any human has ever made.

EricLudy.com

MORE BOOKS FROM ERIC LUDY

Romance, Relationships, & Purity

When God Writes Your Love Story
When Dreams Come True
Meet Mr. Smith
A Perfect Wedding
The First 90 Days of Marriage
Teaching True Love to a Sex-at-13 Generation
It Takes a Gentleman and a Lady

Godly Manhood

God's Gift to Women

Christian Living & Discipleship

When God Writes Your Life Story
The Bravehearted Gospel
Heroism

Prayer

Wrestling Prayer

Memoirs & Confessions

Are These Really My Pants?
Evolution of the Pterodactyl
The Bold Return of the Dunces
Fingerprints of Grace

EricLudy.com

DISCOVER MORE
FROM THE AUTHOR

SERMONS

Unashamed Gospel Thunder.

Listen now: Ellerslie.com/sermons

CONFERENCES

Come expectant. Leave transformed.

Learn more: Ellerslie.com/conferences

DISCIPLESHIP TRAINING

A set apart season to become firmly
planted in Christ.

Learn more: Ellerslie.com/training

READ MORE FROM ERIC LUDY

EricLudy.com

Made in the USA
San Bernardino, CA
26 May 2016